About Insects

Sobre los insectos

For the One who created insects.

—*Genesis* 1:24

Para Aquél que creó a los insectos.

—*Génesis* 1:24

Ω

Published by
PEACHTREE PUBLISHERS
1700 Chattahoochee Avenue
Atlanta, Georgia 30318-2112
www.peachtree-online.com

Text © 2000, 2015 by Cathryn P. Sill
Illustrations © 2000, 2015 by John Sill
Spanish translation © 2015 by Peachtree Publishers

First bilingual edition published in paperback in 2015

Also available in an English-language edition
ISBN 978-1-56145-881-3 (hardcover)
ISBN 978-1-56145-882-0 (paperback)

Spanish translation: Cristina de la Torre
Spanish-language copy editor: Cecilia Molinari

The illustrations were rendered in watercolors

Printed in April 2015 by Imago in China
10 9 8 7 6 5 4 3 2 1 (bilingual hardcover)
10 9 8 7 6 5 4 3 2 1 (bilingual paperback)

Library of Congress Cataloging-in-Publication Data

Sill, Cathryn P., 1953- author.
  About insects : a guide for children = Sobre los insectos : una guía para niños / Cathryn Sill ; illustrated by John Sill ; translated by Cristina de la Torre / ilustraciones de John Sill ; traducción de Cristina de la Torre. — First edition.
    pages cm
  "First bilingual edition published in hardcover and trade paperback in 2015."
  Includes bibliographical references.
  ISBN 978-1-56145-896-7 (hardcover)
  ISBN 978-1-56145-883-7 (paperback)
  1. Insects—Juvenile literature. 2. Insects—Behavior—Juvenile literature. 3. Insects—Anatomy—Juvenile literature. I. Sill, John, illustrator. II. De la Torre, Cristina, translator. III. Sill, Cathryn P., 1953- About insects. IV. Sill, Cathryn P., 1953- About insects. Spanish. V. Title. VI. Title: Sobre los insectos.
  QL467.2.S538 2015
  595.7—dc23
                                        2015002402

About Insects

Sobre los insectos

A Guide for Children / Una guía para niños

Cathryn Sill

Illustrated by / *Ilustraciones de* John Sill

Translated by / *Traducción de* Cristina de la Torre

PEACHTREE

ATLANTA

Insects have six legs...

Los insectos tienen seis patas...

and three body parts.

y tres partes del cuerpo.

PLATE 2 / LÁMINA 2
Eastern Velvet Ant / *hormiga aterciopelada*

They have a waterproof skeleton on the outside of their bodies.

Tienen un esqueleto impermeable en el exterior del cuerpo.

PLATE 3 / LÁMINA 3
Giant Stag Beetle /
ciervo volante gigante

Young insects hatch from eggs.

Las crías nacen de huevos.

PLATE 4 / LÁMINA 4
Praying Mantis / *mantis religiosa*

They go through several changes as they grow up.

Pasan por varios cambios a medida que crecen.

PLATE 5 / LÁMINA 5
Monarch Butterfly / *mariposa monarca*

Antennae help insects smell, taste, and feel.

Los insectos huelen, degustan y sienten con la ayuda de las antenas.

Some insects suck animals or plants to get food.

Algunos insectos se alimentan succionando animales o plantas.

PLATE 7 / LÁMINA 7
Black Horse Fly / *tábano negro*

Others bite and chew their meals.

Otros muerden y mastican sus alimentos.

Many insects fly.

Muchos insectos vuelan.

PLATE 9 / LÁMINA 9
Common Whitetail /
libélula de cola blanca

Some crawl because they have no wings.

Algunos caminan porque no tienen alas.

Others jump...

Otros saltan...

or swim.

o nadan.

PLATE 12 / LÁMINA 12
Whirligig Beetle / *girínido*

Insects live almost everywhere.

En casi todas partes hay insectos.

Some are active during the day.

Algunos están activos durante el día.

PLATE 14 / LÁMINA 14
Honeybee / *abeja*

Others are active only at night.

Otros están activos solamente de noche.

PLATE 15 / LÁMINA 15
Luna Moth / *polilla de luna*

Some insects may be pests.

Algunos insectos pueden ser plagas.

PLATE 16 / LÁMINA 16
German Cockroach /
cucaracha alemana

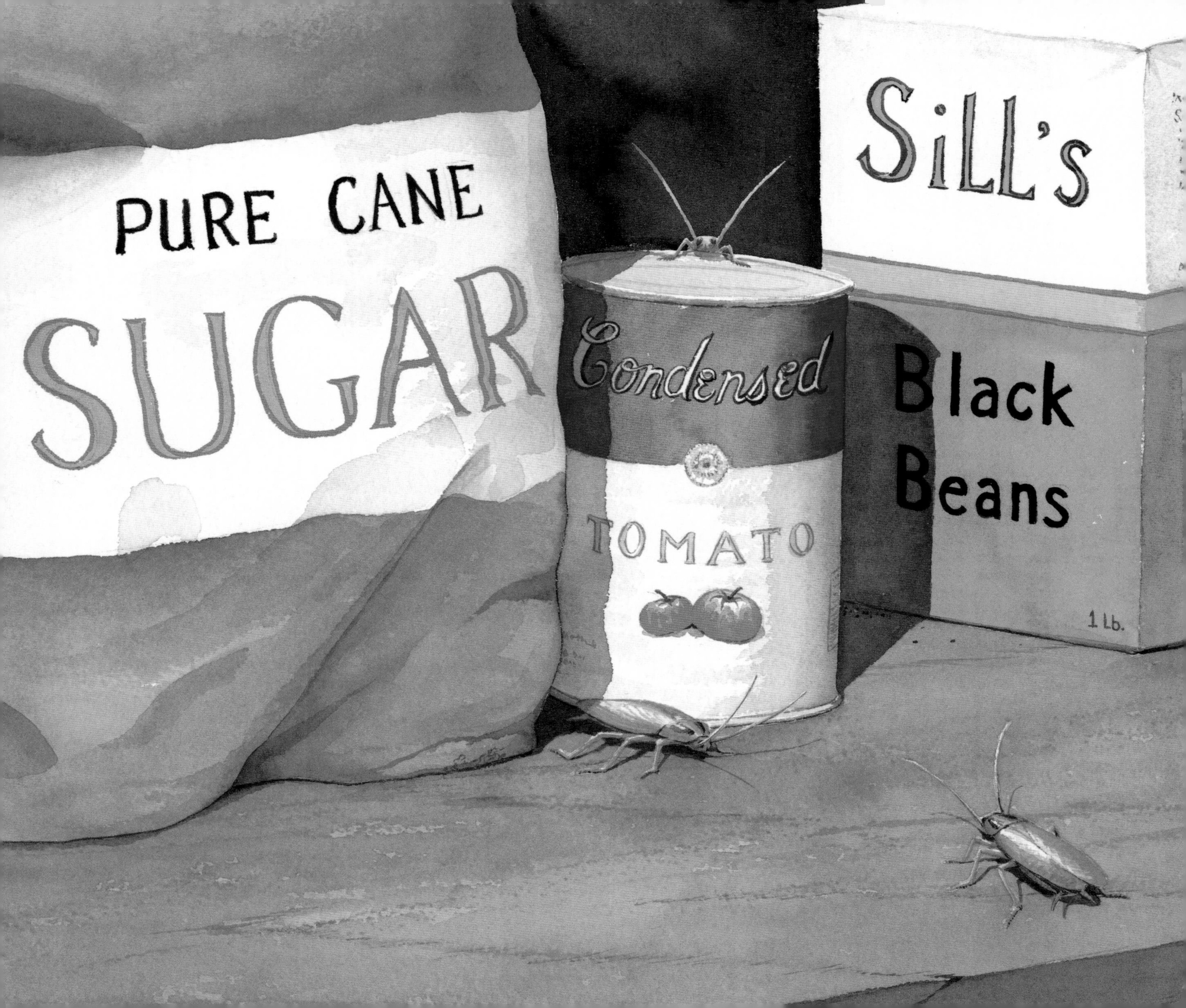
PURE CANE
SUGAR
Condensed
TOMATO
SiLL's
Black
Beans
1 Lb.

But many are very helpful.

Pero muchos son muy útiles.

Insects are an important part of our world.

Los insectos son una parte importante de nuestro mundo.

PLATE 18 / LÁMINA 18
Mayfly / *efímera*

(also shown, Rainbow Trout)
(también en la ilustración, trucha arcoíris)

Afterword / Epílogo

PLATE 1

Insects are found almost everywhere and are the most numerous of all animals. More than 1 million species have been identified. Some experts believe there are 2 million to 30 million insects that have never been discovered and named. Dogbane Leaf Beetles live throughout the eastern United States and southern Canada. They leak a bad-smelling liquid to stay safe from predators.

LÁMINA 1

Los insectos se encuentran en casi todas partes y son los más numerosos de todos los animales. Se han identificado más de un millón de especies. Algunos expertos creen que hay entre 2 y 30 millones de insectos que nunca han sido descubiertos ni nombrados. Los escarabajos de hoja de apocino habitan en el este de Estados Unidos y en el sur de Canadá. Segregan un líquido apestoso para defenderse de sus predadores.

PLATE 2

The three parts of an insect's body are the head, the thorax, and the abdomen. The antennae, eyes, and mouth are located on the head. The legs and wings are attached to the thorax. Organs in the abdomen allow insects to digest food, breathe, and reproduce. Eastern Velvet Ants are antlike wasps with such a painful sting that they are sometimes called "cow killers." They live in the eastern United States.

LÁMINA 2

Las tres partes del cuerpo de un insecto son la cabeza, el tórax y el abdomen. Las antenas, los ojos y la boca están en la cabeza. Las patas y las alas salen del tórax. Los órganos del abdomen les permiten digerir los alimentos, respirar y reproducirse. Las hormigas aterciopeladas son avispas que parecen hormigas y su picada es tan dolorosa que a veces las llaman "matavacas". Viven en el este de Estados Unidos.

PLATE 3

Insects have hard coverings called exoskeletons. "Exo" means "outside." The insect's muscles are attached to the inside of the exoskeleton. Stag beetles get their name from their huge jaws, which look like the antlers of a stag. Males use their jaws for fighting each other. There are about 1,200 species of stag beetles around the world. Giant Stag Beetles live around rotting oak stumps in the eastern United States and west to Oklahoma.

LÁMINA 3

Los insectos poseen capas exteriores duras llamadas exoesqueletos. "Exo" quiere decir "afuera". Los músculos de los insectos se enganchan en el interior del exoesqueleto. Los ciervos volantes se llaman así por sus enormes mandíbulas, que se parecen a las astas de los venados. Los machos usan las mandíbulas para pelearse entre sí. Hay cerca de 1.200 especies de ciervos volantes en todo el mundo. Los ciervos volantes gigantes habitan alrededor de troncos podridos de robles en el este de Estados Unidos, extendiéndose hacia el oeste hasta Oklahoma.

PLATE 4

Insects grow up by a process called "metamorphosis." Some insects go through simple metamorphosis with three stages of growth—egg, nymph, and adult. The female Praying Mantis squeezes a special foam from her body and lays 100 to 200 eggs in the foam. It hardens and protects the eggs until they are ready to hatch. Each egg hatches into a nymph that looks like a tiny version of the adult. Praying Mantises are native to southern Europe. They were first brought to North America in 1889 on a shipment of plants.

PLATE 5

Butterflies and many other insects develop by complete metamorphosis. They go through four stages of development—egg, larva, pupa, and adult. An adult lays an egg that produces a wormlike larva. The larva feeds and grows, then changes into a pupa. When the pupa is fully developed, an adult insect emerges. Monarch Butterflies are the only butterflies that have a two-way migration. They live in most of North America.

PLATE 6

Antennae, which are found on the front of an insect's head, are sometimes called "feelers." They are sense organs that help insects find food and locate enemies. The shape and size of antennae varies for different kinds of insects. Virginia Ctenuchid Moths have feathery antennae. They live in southern Canada and the northern United States.

LÁMINA 4

Los insectos crecen por medio de un proceso llamado "metamorfosis". Algunos pasan por una metamorfosis simple, de tres etapas de crecimiento: huevo, ninfa y adulto. La mantis religiosa hembra segrega una espuma especial de su cuerpo y pone entre 100 y 200 huevos en la espuma, que se endurece y los protege hasta que están listos para romperse. De cada huevito sale una ninfa que es una versión pequeñita idéntica al adulto. Las mantis religiosas son originarias del sur de Europa y llegaron a América del Norte en 1889 en un cargamento de plantas.

LÁMINA 5

Las mariposas, y muchos otros insectos, se desarrollan por medio de una metamorfosis completa, de cuatro etapas: huevo, larva, crisálida y adulto. La hembra adulta pone un huevo que produce una larva parecida a un gusano. La larva come y crece, y entonces se convierte en crisálida. Cuando la crisálida ha terminado su desarrollo emerge el insecto adulto. Las mariposas monarcas son las únicas mariposas que hacen una migración de ida y vuelta. Viven en casi toda América del Norte.

LÁMINA 6

Las antenas, que se encuentran en la parte frontal de la cabeza de los insectos, les sirven para explorar su entorno. Son órganos sensoriales que los insectos usan para encontrar alimentos y detectar a sus enemigos. La forma y el tamaño de las antenas varían según el tipo de insecto. Las polillas de Virginia tienen antenas muy ligeras. Habitan el sur de Canadá y el norte de Estados Unidos.

PLATE 7

Most flies have mouthparts that lap up liquids. Horse fly females suck blood from mammals after slicing the skin with scissor-like mouthparts. Males drink nectar from flowers. There are many kinds of horse flies around the world. Black Horse Flies are common in the eastern United States.

LÁMINA 7

La mayoría de las moscas pueden sorber líquidos con partes de la boca. Los tábanos hembra chupan la sangre de los mamíferos tras cortarles la piel con partes de la boca que son como tijeras. Los machos beben el néctar de las flores. Hay muchos tipos de tábanos en el mundo. Los tábanos negros son comunes en el este de Estados Unidos.

PLATE 8

Insects such as grasshoppers bite and chew their food by moving their mandibles (jaws) from side to side. Grasshoppers live in grasslands, fields, meadows, and forests all over the world. Southeastern Lubber Grasshoppers live on roadsides, in field edges, and in gardens in the southeastern United States.

LÁMINA 8

Algunos insectos, tales como los saltamontes, muerden y mastican los alimentos moviendo las mandíbulas (las quijadas) de un lado a otro. Los saltamontes viven en pastizales, campos, praderas y bosques en todas partes del mundo. Los saltamontes del sudeste se encuentran al borde de carreteras y campos, y en los jardines del sudeste de Estados Unidos.

PLATE 9

Most adult insects have two pairs of wings attached to the thorax. Some insects have only one pair of wings. Dragonflies have four wings that move independently, enabling them to fly backward as well as forward. Common Whitetails catch and eat small insects while in flight. They are found through most of the United States and southern Canada.

LÁMINA 9

La mayoría de los insectos adultos tienen dos pares de alas pegadas al tórax. Algunos insectos tienen solamente un par de alas. Las libélulas tienen cuatro alas que se mueven independientemente y les permiten volar hacia delante o hacia atrás. Las libélulas de cola blanca capturan y comen pequeños insectos mientras vuelan. Se encuentran en casi todas partes de Estados Unidos y en el sur de Canadá.

PLATE 10

Some insects mimic parts of the plants on which they live. Giant Walkingsticks look so much like twigs that predators easily overlook them. Measuring nearly six inches (150 cm), they are the longest insects in North America. Giant Walkingsticks live in the southeastern and midwestern United States.

LÁMINA 10

Algunos insectos imitan partes de las plantas en las que viven. Los insectos palo gigantes son tan similares a ramitas que suelen pasar inadvertidos por sus predadores. Miden alrededor de seis pulgadas (150 cm), lo cual los hace los insectos más largos de América del Norte. Los insectos palo gigantes habitan en el sudeste y el medio oeste de Estados Unidos.

PLATE 11

Strong muscles in their back legs help some insects jump long distances. Many insects that jump make sounds by rubbing one body part against another. Katydids and crickets "sing" by raising their wings and rubbing them together. Gladiator Meadow Katydids live in the northern half of the United States and in southern Canada.

LÁMINA 11

Algunos tipos de insectos pueden saltar largas distancias gracias a los fuertes músculos de sus patas traseras. Muchos de los insectos saltarines hacen ruidos frotando una parte del cuerpo contra otra. Las esperanzas y los grillos "cantan" alzando las alas y frotándolas entre sí. Las esperanzas gladiadoras viven en el norte de Estados Unidos y en el sur de Canadá.

PLATE 12

Beetles that live in lakes, ponds, rivers, and streams have paddle-shaped back legs that help them swim. Whirligig Beetles swim around on the surface of the water. They can also fly and dive underwater. Whirligig Beetles' eyes are divided into two parts so they are able to see above and below the surface of the water. There are around 700 species of Whirligig Beetles around the world. They live throughout North America.

LÁMINA 12

Los escarabajos que viven en lagos, estanques, ríos y arroyos tienen las patas traseras en forma de paletas que los ayudan a nadar. Los girínidos se deslizan sobre la superficie del agua, y también son capaces de sumergirse y de volar. Los girínidos tienen los ojos divididos en dos partes para poder ver sobre y debajo de la superficie del agua. Hay alrededor de 700 especies de girínidos en el mundo y se encuentran por toda América del Norte.

PLATE 13

Insects are found in almost every habitat on the earth, but very few of them are able to live in the salty water in oceans. Silverfish are found all over the world in warm, moist places. Outdoors they live under fallen leaves, rocks, and logs. Indoors they are found in attics, basements, behind furniture, and near sinks or bathtubs. They eat many things, including plants, clothing, dry foods, paper, and book bindings.

LÁMINA 13

En casi todos los hábitats de la tierra hay insectos, pero muy pocos pueden vivir en las aguas saladas de los océanos. Los pececillos plateados se encuentran en sitios templados y húmedos alrededor del mundo. En el exterior se encuentran bajo hojas caídas, piedras y troncos. En el interior se encuentran en áticos, sótanos, detrás de muebles, y cerca de lavabos o bañeras. Comen una variedad de cosas, incluyendo plantas, ropa, alimentos secos, papel y encuadernación de libros.

PLATE 14

Animals that are active in the daytime are called "diurnal." Honeybees live in colonies or large groups that work together. The worker bees spend warm days gathering food from flowers. They eat pollen and nectar. Honeybees use nectar to make honey to eat in winter when flowers are not blooming. Settlers brought honeybees to North America from Europe during the 1600s.

LÁMINA 14

Los animales activos durante el día se llaman "diurnos". Las abejas viven en colonias o grandes grupos que trabajan juntos. Las abejas obreras pasan los días cálidos recolectando alimento de las flores. Comen polen y néctar. Las abejas usan el néctar para elaborar la miel que las alimenta durante el invierno cuando las plantas no están florecidas. Los colonos europeos trajeron las abejas a las Américas en el siglo XVII.

PLATE 15

Most moths are nocturnal (active at night). Luna Moth caterpillars eat tree leaves. Adults do not eat at all. They reproduce and then die. Luna Moths were once common but are now rare because of insecticides and pollutants. They live in North America east of the Great Plains.

LÁMINA 15

La mayoría de las polillas son nocturnas (activas durante la noche). Las orugas de la polilla de luna se alimentan de las hojas de los árboles. Las adultas no comen nada. Se reproducen y mueren. Hubo una época en que las polillas de luna eran comunes pero hoy día no abundan debido a los insecticidas y las sustancias contaminantes. Viven en zonas al este de los Grandes Llanos en América del Norte.

PLATE 16

Insects are considered pests when they annoy or harm people. Some insects can destroy valuable crops, have irritating bites or stings, carry disease, infest food supplies, or damage wooden buildings. German Cockroaches have an unpleasant odor and search for food in homes, restaurants, and food factories. They live all over the world wherever people live.

LÁMINA 16

Los insectos se consideran plagas cuando molestan o hacen daño a las personas. Algunos insectos son capaces de destruir valiosos cultivos, otros tienen picadas o mordidas irritantes, transmiten enfermedades, infectan las reservas de alimentos o dañan las edificaciones de madera. Las cucarachas alemanas tienen un olor desagradable y buscan alimentos en los hogares, restaurantes y fábricas de alimentos. Se encuentran en cualquier lugar del mundo donde hay seres humanos.

PLATE 17

Many insects help humans by eating other insects that destroy crops. Lady beetle (also called "ladybug") larvae and adults eat aphids and other small insects. Farmers and gardeners often buy lady beetles and turn them loose near crops that are harmed by aphids. Convergent Lady Beetles are common throughout North America and parts of South America.

LÁMINA 17

Muchos insectos ayudan a los humanos ya que se alimentan de otros insectos que destruyen cultivos. Las larvas de mariquitas, así como las adultas, se alimentan de áfidos y otros insectos pequeños. Muchos granjeros y jardineros compran mariquitas y las sueltan cerca de los cultivos que los áfidos atacan. Las mariquitas son comunes en toda América del Norte y partes de América del Sur.

PLATE 18

Insects are an important food source for animals. They pollinate many of the plants that provide food for us. Insects produce useful products such as honey, beeswax, and silk. Some people enjoy watching insects and learning about their habits. Mayfly nymphs live in clean fresh water. As they become adults, they leave the water and grow wings. There are thousands of kinds of mayflies around the world and hundreds in North America.

LÁMINA 18

Los insectos son una fuente importante de alimento para los animales. Polinizan muchas de las plantas que nos sirven de alimento a nosotros. Los insectos nos proveen productos útiles como la miel, la cera y la seda. Algunas personas disfrutan observando a los insectos y aprendiendo sobre sus hábitos. Las efímeras habitan en aguas dulces limpias. Al hacerse adultas salen del agua y les crecen las alas. Hay miles de tipos de efímeras en todo el mundo y cientos de ellos en América del Norte.

GLOSSARY

habitat—the place where animals and plants live
insecticide—a chemical used to kill insects
organ—a part of an animal's body that does a specific job (for example, eyes, lungs, heart)
pollutant—anything that makes water, air, or land unclean or impure
predator—an animal that lives by hunting and eating other animals
reproduce—to have babies
species—a group of animals or plants that are alike in many ways
true bug—an insect with sucking, beaklike mouthparts
two-way migration—the movement of an animal from its birthplace to a warmer place for winter and then back in summer.

GLOSARIO

hábitat: lugar en que viven animales y plantas
insecticida: producto químico usado para matar insectos
órgano: parte del cuerpo de un animal que tiene una función específica (por ejemplo, los ojos, los pulmones, el corazón)
contaminante: cualquier cosa que ensucia o poluciona el agua, el aire o la tierra
predador: animal que sobrevive cazando y comiendo otros animales
reproducirse: tener crías
especie: grupo de animales o plantas que son muy semejantes
chinche: insecto con piezas bucales que tienen forma de pico y sirven para succionar
migración de ida y vuelta: movimiento de animales entre el lugar donde nacieron a sitios más cálidos durante el invierno y de regreso en el verano.

BIBLIOGRAPHY

BOOKS

Insects: (Golden Guide) by Clarence Cottam and Herbert Zim (St. Martin's Press)
Kaufman Field Guide to Insects of North America by Eric R. Eaton and Kenn Kaufman (Houghton Mifflin)
Peterson First Guide to Insects of North America by Christopher Leahy (Houghton Mifflin)

WEBSITES

www.insectidentification.org
www.biokids.umich.edu/critters/Insecta
www.bugfacts.net/index.php#.U4TiBCibLVo

ABOUT... SERIES

ISBN 978-1-56145-234-7 HC
ISBN 978-1-56145-312-2 PB

ISBN 978-1-56145-038-1 HC
ISBN 978-1-56145-364-1 PB

ISBN 978-1-56145-688-8 HC
ISBN 978-1-56145-699-4 PB

ISBN 978-1-56145-301-6 HC
ISBN 978-1-56145-405-1 PB

ISBN 978-1-56145-256-9 HC
ISBN 978-1-56145-335-1 PB

ISBN 978-1-56145-588-1 HC
ISBN 978-1-56145-837-0 PB

ISBN 978-1-56145-881-3 HC
ISBN 978-1-56145-882-0 PB

ISBN 978-1-56145-757-1 HC
ISBN 978-1-56145-758-8 PB

ISBN 978-1-56145-358-0 HC
ISBN 978-1-56145-407-5 PB

ISBN 978-1-56145-331-3 HC
ISBN 978-1-56145-406-8 PB

ISBN 978-1-56145-795-3 HC

ISBN 978-1-56145-743-4 HC
ISBN 978-1-56145-741-0 PB

ISBN 978-1-56145-536-2 HC
ISBN 978-1-56145-811-0 PB

ISBN 978-1-56145-183-8 HC
ISBN 978-1-56145-233-0 PB

ISBN 978-1-56145-454-9 HC

**ALSO AVAILABLE
IN BILINGUAL EDITION**

**TAMBIÉN DISPONIBLES
EN EDICIÓN BILINGÜE**

- About Birds / Sobre los pájaros
  ISBN 978-1-56145-783-0 PB
- About Mammals / Sobre los mamíferos
  ISBN 978-1-56145-800-4 PB
- About Insects / Sobre los insectos
  ISBN 978-1-56145-883-7 PB

ABOUT HABITATS SERIES

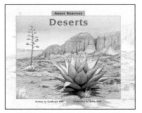

Deserts

ISBN 978-1-56145-641-3 HC
ISBN 978-1-56145-636-9 PB

Forests

ISBN 978-1-56145-734-2 HC

Grasslands

ISBN 978-1-56145-559-1 HC

Mountains

ISBN 978-1-56145-469-3 HC
ISBN 978-1-56145-731-1 PB

Oceans

ISBN 978-1-56145-618-5 HC

Polar Regions

ISBN 978-1-56145-832-5 HC

Wetlands

ISBN 978-1-56145-432-7 HC
ISBN 978-1-56145-689-5 PB

THE SILLS

CATHRYN AND JOHN SILL are the dynamic team who created the *About…* series as well as the *About Habitats* series. Their books have garnered praise from educators and have won a variety of awards, including Bank Street Best Books, CCBC Choices, NSTA/CBC Outstanding Science Trade Books for Students K–12, Orbis Pictus Recommended, and *Science Books and Films* Best Books of the Year. Cathryn, a graduate of Western Carolina State University, taught early elementary school classes for thirty years. John holds a BS in wildlife biology from North Carolina State University. Combining his artistic skill and knowledge of wildlife, he has achieved an impressive reputation as a wildlife artist. The Sills live in Franklin, North Carolina.

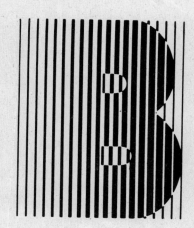

Student's Book

SPELLING
MASTERY
a direct instruction series

Level B

Robert Dixon
Siegfried Engelmann
Mary Meier

PERGAMON

SCIENCE RESEARCH ASSOCIATES, INC.
Chicago, Henley-on-Thames, Sydney, Toronto
A Maxwell Pergamon Publishing Company

ISBN   0-574-72132-0

Lesson 1

Part a

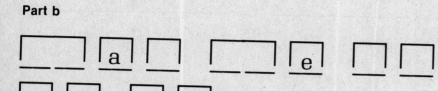

What are we to do?

Part b

☐☐ a ☐ ☐☐ e ☐ ☐

☐ o ☐ ☐ **?**

Part c

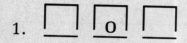

1. ☐ o ☐

2. ☐ ☐ ☐

3. ☐ ☐ i n g

4. ☐ o i n g

5. ☐ i ☐

Part d

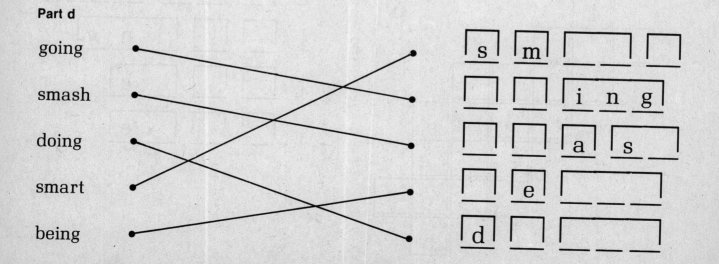

going

smash

doing

smart

being

s m ☐ ☐

☐ ☐ i n g

☐ ☐ a s

☐ e ☐

d ☐ ☐

Lesson 2

Part a

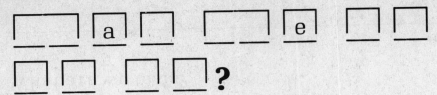

[□][□] [a][□]   [□][□] [e] [□][□]

[□][□] [□][□] ?

Part b

1. _____

2. _____

Part c

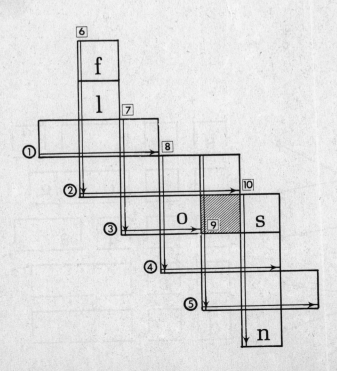

Part d

1.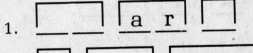

2.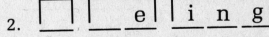

3.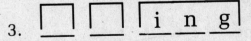

4. [□][□][□ e]

5. [□][□][□ e]

Lesson 3

Part a

1. tar   2. hard   3. part   4. mark   5. card

Part b

☐ ☐ ☐ ☐ ☐ ☐ ☐ ☐

☐ ☐ ☐ ☐ **?**

Part c

She has many friends.

Part d

☐ ☐ ☐ ☐ ☐ ☐ a ☐ y

☐ ☐ i e ☐ ☐ ☐ .

Part e

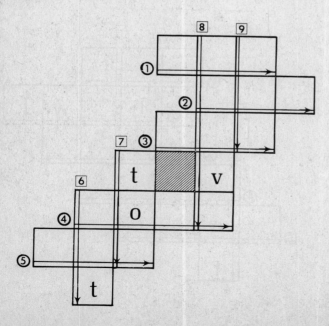

Lesson 4

Part a

1. dark   2. sharp   3. arm   4. charm   5. car

Part b

1. _____

2. _____

Part c

☐☐ ☐ ☐☐ ☐☐ s ☐ a ☐ ☐

☐ ☐ i e ☐ ☐ ☐ .

_____

Part d

1. s e e ☐ ☐ ☐   4. ☐ a r k

2. ☐ ☐ a r ☐   5. ☐ ☐ a r ☐

3. ☐ ☐ a ☐

Part e

1. The boy was angry.
   He was _____.

2. I eat my cereal from
   a _____.

3. The opposite of hate
   is _____.

4. Birds don't _____ fur.

5. Seal the package with
   _____.

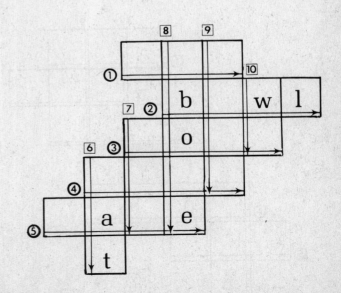

Lesson 5

Part a

1. dull   2. fell   3. hill   4. fill   5. smell

Part b

1. _____

2. _____

3. _____

Part c

☐ ☐ ☐ ☐ ☐ ☐ ☐ ☐ ☐
☐ ☐ ☐ ☐ ☐ ☐ ☐ .

Part d

1. Last night, we wished upon a _____.

2. The opposite of hard is _____.

3. At Christmas, many people _____ gifts to each other.

4. The last part of the story is the _____.

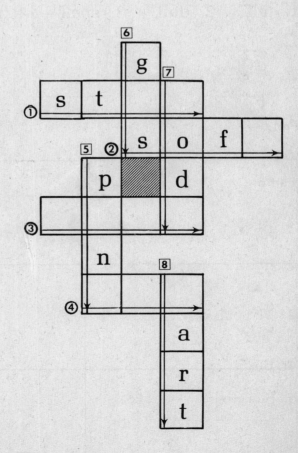

Lesson 6

Part a

1. _____

2. _____

3. _____

Part b

1. tell   2. dull   3. spell   4. mill   5. pill

Part c

Lesson 7

Part a

1. _____

2. _____

Part b

_____

Will you come with us?

Part c

□ □ □   □ o □   □ o □ □

□ □ □   □ □ ?

Part d

1. | p | | t | | |

2. | | | |

3. | d | o | |

4. | | o | |

Lesson 8

Part a

1. salt   2. call   3. fall   4. bald   5. also

Part b

☐ ☐ ☐ ☐ ☐o☐ ☐o☐ ☐
☐ ☐ ☐ ☐☐ **?**

_____

Part c

1. _____   6. _____
2. _____   7. _____
3. _____   8. _____
4. _____   9. _____
5. _____   10. _____

Part d

1. _____

2. _____

Lesson 9

Part a

1. also   2. ball   3. bald   4. salt   5. hall

Part b

1. _____

2. _____

3. _____

Part c

☐ ☐ ☐ ☐   ☐ ☐ ☐   ☐ ☐ ☐ ☐

☐ ☐ ☐ ☐   ☐ ☐ **?**

_____

Part d

Lesson 10

Part a

1. _____

2. _____

Part b

_____

They read part of the book.

Part c

☐ ☐ e ☐   ☐ ☐ a ☐   ☐ ☐ ☐ ☐

☐ f ☐ ☐ ☐   ☐ ☐ ☐ ☐ .

Part d

1. He went from his house
   _____ the store.

2. Rain turned the
   dirt into _____.

3. The first prize went for
   the _____ picture.

4. The angry man was
   _____ happy.

5. Seven children _____
   in that house.

6. The pillow _____ soft.

Lesson 11

Part a

1. _____

2. _____

Part b

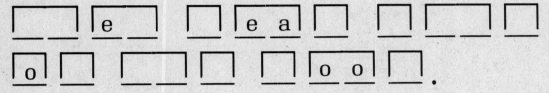

```
[ ][ ][e][ ]   [ ][e][a][ ]   [ ][ ][ ][ ]
[o][ ]   [ ][ ][ ]   [ ][o][o][ ].
```

Part c

1. Hold on tightly or you might _____.

2. She rang the school _____.

3. She had a _____ in the play.

4. Don't knock. _____ the doorbell.

5. He trained his dog to _____ his shoes.

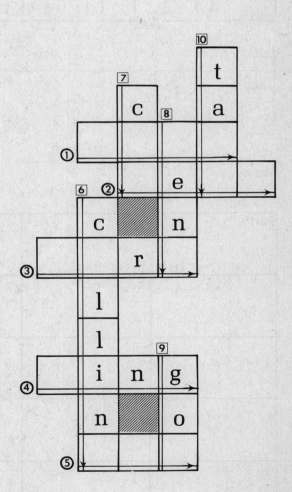

Lesson 12

Part a

1. _____

2. _____

Part b

☐ ☐ ☐ ☐ ☐ ☐ ☐ ☐ ☐ ☐ ☐
— — — — — — — — — — —

☐ ☐ ☐ ☐ ☐ ☐ .
— — — — — —

Part c

Lesson 13

Part a

1. love   4. dove   7. above

2. some   5. glove   8. none

3. done   6. one   9. shove

Part b

1. _____

2. _____

Part c

Where were the girls going?

_____

Part d

1. friends

2. what

3. none

4. done

5. doing

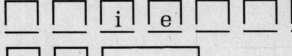
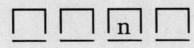
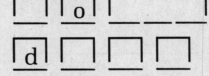
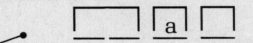

Lesson 14

Part a

1. _____   4. _____

2. _____   5. _____

3. _____

Part b

1. _____   5. _____

2. _____   6. _____

3. _____   7. _____

4. _____

Part c

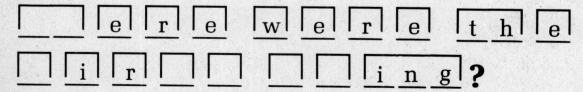

___ e r e   w e r e   t h e

___ i r ___ ___ ___ ___ i n g ?

_____

Lesson 15

Part a

1. _____

2. _____

Part b

Thay gave us meny buks.

Part c

1. _____   4. _____

2. _____   5. _____

3. _____   6. _____

Part d

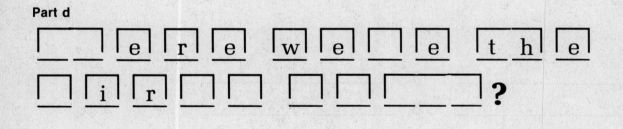

Part e

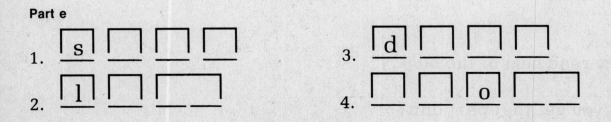

Lesson 16

Part a

☐☐ e ☐ r ☐ e ☐☐☐ ☐☐ ☐

☐ i ☐ r ☐☐ ☐ ☐☐☐☐ **?**

_____

Part b

1. _____

2. _____

Part c

1. _____   5. _____

2. _____   6. _____

3. _____   7. _____

4. _____

Part d

1. They read sum of the book.

2. Did you get that part dun?

Lesson 17

Part a

☐ ☐ e r e ☐ ☐ ☐ ☐ ☐ ☐
☐ ☐ ☐ ☐ ☐ ☐ ☐ ☐ ?

_____

Part b

1. _____

2. _____

3. _____

Part c

1. The shelf is abuv the desk.

2. Nun of the cake was left.

Part d

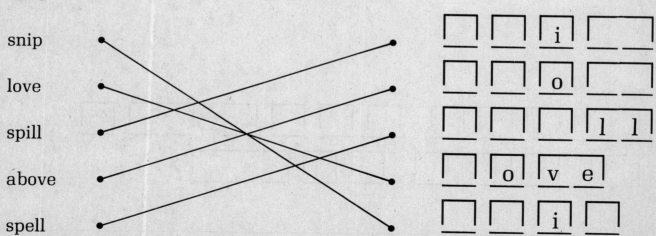

snip

love

spill

above

spell

Lesson 18

Part a

1. _____

2. _____

Part b

1. _____   4. _____

2. _____   5. _____

3. _____   6. _____

Part c

1. _____   4. _____

2. _____   5. _____

3. _____

Part d

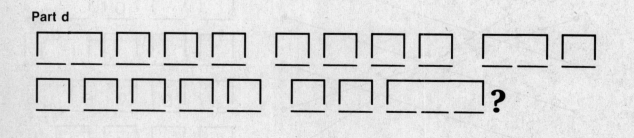

Lesson 19

Part a

1. _____

2. _____

Part b

1. _____   4. _____

2. _____   5. _____

3. _____

Part c

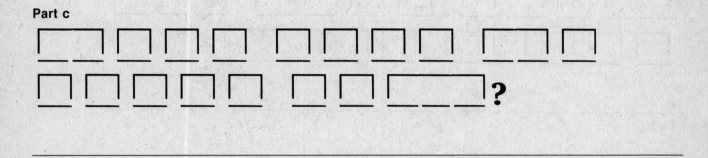

Part d

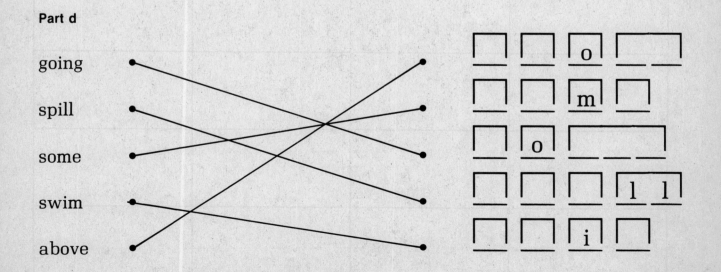

Lesson 20

Part a

1. _____

2. _____

Part b

1. He gave a hard shuv.

2. Can I have wun?

Part c

□□□ □ □□ □ □□□□ □ □□ □

□□□□□ □□□□□?

_____

Part d

Lesson 21

Part a

_____

Part b

Where wer the gluvz?

Part c

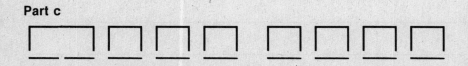

☐☐☐☐ ☐☐☐☐ ☐☐☐
___ ___ ___ ___   ___ ___ ___ ___   ___ ___ ___

☐☐☐☐☐ ☐☐☐☐?
___ ___ ___ ___ ___   ___ ___ ___

_____

Part d

1. ☐ a n
   ___

2. ☐ i n
   ___

3. ☐ o t
   ___

4. ☐ u p
   ___

5. ☐ e g
   ___

Part e

1. _____   2. _____   3. _____

Lesson 22

Part a

1. _____   3. _____   5. _____

2. _____   4. _____

Part b

1. _____

2. _____

Part c

1. _____   3. _____   5. _____

2. _____   4. _____

Part d

Wair was that duv?

Part e

slop   •   • ☐ ☐ o p

stop   •   • ☐ ☐ a p

snap   •   • s n ☐ ☐

snip   •   • ☐ ☐ i p

slip   •   • s l ☐ ☐

Lesson 23

Part a

1. _____   4. _____

2. _____   5. _____

3. _____   6. _____

Part b

Even he had enough.

_____

Part c

1. _____   5. _____

2. _____   6. _____

3. _____   7. _____

4. _____   8. _____

Part d

clap   •   •   ☐ ☐ a ☐

girls •   •   g ☐ ☐ ☐

snap   •   •   ☐ i ☐

kin   •   •   ☐ i ☐ ☐ ☐

glove •   •   ☐ l ☐ ☐

Lesson 24

Part a

1. _____

2. _____

Part b

1. _____   4. _____

2. _____   5. _____

3. _____

Part c

E v e n ☐ ☐ ☐ ☐ ☐

e n o u g h .

Part d

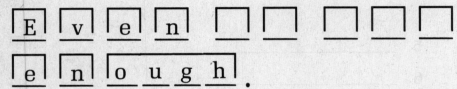

stem •

where •

smart •

were •

seeing •

Lesson 25

Part a

1. begin   2. began   3. behind   4. below   5. rerun

Part b

1. _____   5. _____   9. _____

2. _____   6. _____   10. _____

3. _____   7. _____

4. _____   8. _____

Part c

_____

Part d

☐ ☐ ☐ ☐ ☐ ☐ ☐ ☐ ☐
___ ___ ___ ___ ___ ___ ___ ___ ___

| e | n | | o | u | g | h |.

_____

Part e

snip   •

clap   •

where   •

spell   •

swim   •

•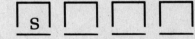

•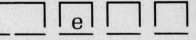

•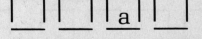

•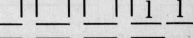

Part a

Wur the kites ubuv the trees?

I hav a smal kut on my hand.

Part b

_____

Part c

1. even

2. rerun

3. behind

4. below

Part d

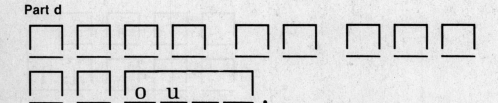

_____

Part a

1. retell
2. depart
3. resell

Part b

1. _____
2. _____
3. _____
4. _____

Part c

□ □ □ □ □ □ □ □ □
□ □ □‾‾‾‾‾ .

Part d

love •

were •

none •

where •

many •

• □ o □ e

• □ □ e r e

• □ □ □ □

• □ e r e

• □ □ v e

Lesson 28

Part a

1. _____   3. _____

2. _____   4. _____

Part b

1. _____

2. _____

Part c

She had enuf.

Part d

1. _____   4. _____

2. _____   5. _____

3. _____   6. _____

Part e

cat •   • [ ][ ][t]

can •   • [ ][ ][a][n]

kin •   • [ ][a][ ]

kit •   • [ ][a][t]

clan •   • [ ][ ][n]

Lesson 29

Part a

Part b

1. The teacher was
   _____ the
   boxes with labels.

2. When he comes on stage,
   everyone will _____.

3. When you open your eyes,
   you can _____.

4. Many people wear
   _____ to keep
   their heads warm.

5. She used to spray to _____
   the weeds.

6. I just read a good _____.

7. When the light turns red,
   you must _____.

8. He used a masher to _____
   the potatoes.

9. He took off the bottle _____.

10. The bird was high _____
    the ocean.

11. A roof is on _____ of a house.

12. The tree was _____ weak that
    it fell over.

13. The table _____ yellow.

14. She wrapped the scarf around
    her _____.

15. You can tell the _____ of a tree
    by counting its rings.

Lesson 30

Do you have blue shoes?

_____

Part b

1. _____   5. _____

2. _____   6. _____

3. _____   7. _____

4. _____   8. _____

Part c

1. _____

2. _____

Part d

gram   •   • | t | r | | |

trim   •   • | | | i | m |

brim   •   • | | | a | t |

brat   •   • | b | r | | |

prim   •   • | | | | |

Part a

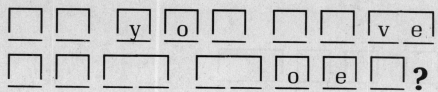

_____

Part b

1. _____

2. _____

3. _____

4. _____

5. _____

6. _____

Part c

1. [ ] [a] [ ]

2. [ ] [u] [ ]

3. [ ] [i] [ ]

4. [ ] [o] [ ]

5. [ ] [e] [ ]

Lesson 32

Part a

☐ ☐ ☐y ☐o☐ ☐ ☐ ☐ ☐
☐ ☐ ☐u e☐ ☐ ☐o☐e☐ ☐ **?**

_____

Part b

1. _____   4. _____

2. _____   5. _____

3. _____   6. _____

Part c

done •

none •

shove •

love •

dove •

• ☐ ☐ ☐o ☐v ☐e

• ☐ ☐o ☐v e☐

• ☐d ☐ ☐ ☐

• ☐ ☐o ☐n ☐e

• ☐l ☐ ☐

Lesson 33

Part a

1. enough   2. rough   3. tough

Part b

1. _____

2. _____

Part c

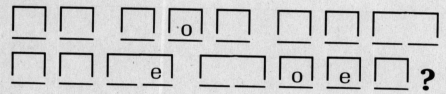

☐ ☐ ☐ o☐ ☐ ☐ ☐ ☐

☐ ☐ ☐ e☐ ☐ o☐ e☐ ?

_____

Part d

smell   •   •   s☐ ☐ ☐

drip   •   •   d☐ ☐ ☐

snip   •   •   ☐ ☐ ☐ p

drag   •   •   ☐ ☐ ☐ e☐ l☐ l☐

resell •   •   s☐ ☐ ☐ ☐

Lesson 34

Part a

1. _____

2. _____

3. _____

Part b

1. _____

2. _____

3. _____

Part c

1. _____   4. _____

2. _____   5. _____

3. _____   6. _____

Part d

⬚ ⬚ ⬚ o⬚ ⬚ ⬚ ⬚ ⬚

⬚ ⬚ e⬚ ⬚ o⬚ e⬚ **?**

Lesson 35

Part a

1. _____ 4. _____

2. _____ 5. _____

3. _____ 6. _____

Part b

⬜⬜ ⬜⬜⬜ ⬜⬜⬜
⬜⬜⬜ ⬜⬜⬜⬜ **?**

_____

Part c

_____

Part d

The gluv is small.

Lesson 36

Part a

1. _____

2. _____

Part b

He gave a ruf shuv.

Part c

1. _____   4. _____

2. _____   5. _____

3. _____   6. _____

Part d

Part e

☐ ☐ ☐ ☐ ☐ ☐ ☐ ☐
___ ___ ___ ___ ___ ___ ___ ___
☐ ☐ ☐ ☐ ☐ ☐ ☐ ☐ **?**
___ ___ ___ ___ ___ ___ ___ ___

Lesson 37

Part a

1. _____

2. _____

3. _____

4. _____

Part b

My frend has a blue kat.

We hav enuf cake.

Part c

1.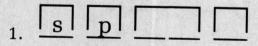

Lesson 38

Part a

1. _____   5. _____

2. _____   6. _____

3. _____   7. _____

4. _____

Part b

1. _____

2. _____

Part c

Where were the bloo shooz **?**

Part d

toy   •   • ☐ [o] [y]

boil   •   • ☐ [o] [i] ☐ ☐

broil   •   • [b] ☐ ☐

joint   •   • [t] ☐

boy   •   • [b] ☐ ☐ ☐

Lesson 39

Part a

1. blue   2. true   3. clue   4. glue

Part b

1. _____

2. _____

Part c

The food started to spoyl.

Part d

1. The girl bounced the
   _____ on the floor.

2. The knife is not dull.
   It is _____.

3. Part of the word
   windmill is _____.

4. A door is part _____
   a house.

5. Do you _____ in that house?

6. Do it by your_____.

7. She scratched because she had
   a _____.

8. The _____ of her clock wakes
   her in the morning.

9. Twice a day he gives the dog a
   vitamin _____.

10. Ice cream _____ cold.

11. Hate is the opposite
    of _____.

12. The snow _____ cold.

Lesson 40

Part a

Is that good enuf?

Part b

Part c

We saw these goats eat weeds.

_____

Part d

1. _____ 7. _____

2. _____ 8. _____

3. _____ 9. _____

4. _____ 10. _____

5. _____ 11. _____

6. _____ 12. _____

Part a

1. _____

2. _____

Part b

The meat was tuf.

Part c

☐ ☐ ☐ [a] [w] ☐ ☐ [e] [s] [e]

☐ [o] [a] ☐ ☐ [e] [a] ☐ ☐ [e] [e] ☐ ☐ .

Part d

joy   •   •   ☐ [o] [y]

point   •   •   ☐ [o] [i] ☐ ☐

join   •   •   [j] ☐ ☐

joint   •   •   [j] ☐

boy   •   •   [p] ☐ ☐ ☐

Lesson 42

Part a

☐ ☐ ☐ a ☐ ☐ ☐ ☐ e
☐ ☐ a ☐ ☐ ☐ ☐ ☐ e ☐ ☐ ☐ .

_____

Part b

1. _____   4. _____

2. _____   5. _____

3. _____   6. _____

Part c

1. ☐ ☐ ☐ ☐ ☐

2. ☐ ☐ ☐ ☐

3. ☐ ☐ ☐ ☐ ☐

4. ☐ ☐ ☐ ☐ ☐

5. ☐ ☐ ☐ ☐ ☐ ☐

Lesson 43

Part a

1. leader   3. repeat   5. neat   7. real   9. year

2. leaf   4. leave   6. reach   8. speak   10. read

Part b

1. _____

2. _____

Part c

☐ ☐ ☐ a ☐ ☐ ☐ ☐ e

☐ ☐ a ☐ ☐ ☐ a ☐ ☐ e ☐ ☐ ☐ .

Part d

Lesson 44

Part a

1. real   3. speak   5. repeat   7. leader   9. reach

2. read   4. leave   6. neat   8. year   10. leaf

Part b

1. _____

2. _____

Part c

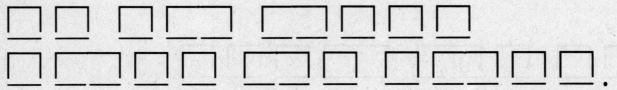

_____

Part d

1. She put groceries in her shopping _____.

2. The opposite of bottom is _____.

3. A ghost came up out of the _____.

4. She was tired and sat down to _____.

5. Be careful not to _____ on the ice.

6. All his children were _____.

7. _____ is black, sticky stuff.

8. The balloon sailed _____ the crowd.

9. A rat is a _____ to farmers.

10. We liked the story a _____.

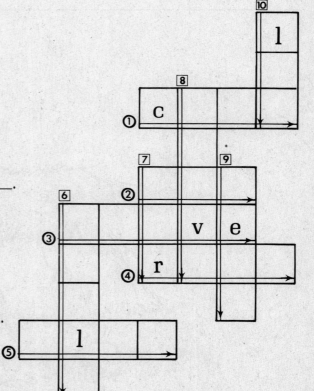

Lesson 45

Part a

1. _____   5. _____

2. _____   6. _____

3. _____   7. _____

4. _____   8. _____

Part b

1. _____

2. _____

3. _____

Part c

1. Goldfish are _____ fish.

2. She _____ the candle with the match.

3. He went to sleep in his _____.

4. The boy lost his grip and _____.

5. My father's mother is my _____mother.

6. The water came from a deep _____.

7. The duck has a yellow _____.

8. I'm going to _____ my money so I can buy a new bicycle.

9. We're going to _____ a hole.

10. That tree is almost as _____ as our house.

11. He threw the ball as _____ as he could.

12. He missed the bus and was _____ for school.

Lesson 46

Did you find a kloo **?**

They red part of the bloo book.

Do you have enuf gloo **?**

Part b

1. _____   4. _____

2. _____   5. _____

3. _____   6. _____

Part c

1. _____

2. _____

3. _____

Part d

broil   •

enough   •

below   •

rough   •

shoes   •

Lesson 47

Part a

1. to   2. do   3. who

Part b

1. _____

2. _____

Part c

1. _____   5. _____

2. _____   6. _____

3. _____   7. _____

4. _____   8. _____

Part d

Lesson 48

Part a

1. _____ 2. _____ 3. _____

Part b

She should put it away.

_____

Part c

1. _____
2. _____

Part d

girl   •   • ☐ ☐ ☐ ☐

spell   •   • r ☐ ☐

boil   •   • s ☐ ☐

real   •   • ☐ ☐ ☐ ☐

fill   •   • m ☐ ☐

salt   •   • f ☐ ☐

meal   •   • b ☐ ☐

soil   •   • ☐ a ☐

Lesson 49

Part a

☐ _ _ ☐ _ _ ☐ _ _ ☐ o _ u _ l ☐ _ ☐ _ ☐ _ u _ ☐

☐ ☐ _ a ☐ _ ☐ _ y .

_____

Part b

1. _____

2. _____

Part c

1. The bats lived in the _____.

2. Don't ask a question. _____ me the answer.

3. They made up a _____ of things to buy.

4. Put a _____ next to the right answer.

5. The opposite of first is _____.

6. Watch out or that bee will _____ you.

7. The opposite of stupid is _____.

8. Is she as tall _____ she looks?

9. They lined up and were ready to _____ the race.

10. Use the telephone to _____ your mother.

Lesson 50

Part a

1. _____   2. _____   3. _____

Part b

1. _____

2. _____

Part c

☐ ☐ ☐ [o] [u] [l] ☐ ☐ ☐ ☐

☐ ☐ ☐ ☐ [y] .

_____

Part d

drum •   • ☐ ☐ ☐ [m]

true •   • ☐ ☐ ☐

love •   • ☐ [l] ☐

trim •   • ☐ [r] ☐

clue •   • ☐ ☐ [u] [m]

Lesson 51

Part a

1. ☐ k ☐ ☐ ☐ e t

2. ☐ c ☐ ☐ ☐ e r

3. ☐ ☐ o u l ☐

4. ☐ ☐ ☐

Part b

1. _____

2. _____

Part c

1. _____   4. _____

2. _____   5. _____

3. _____   6. _____

Part d

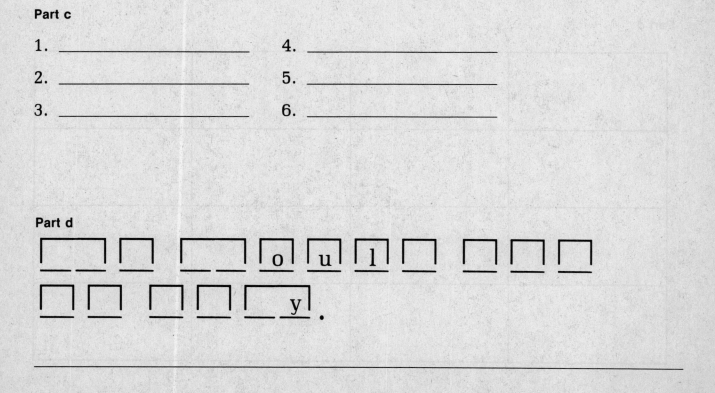

☐ ☐ ☐ ☐ ☐ o u l ☐ ☐ ☐ ☐

☐ ☐ ☐ ☐ y .

_____

Lesson 52

Part a

1. ☐ ☐ ☐ ☐ e t
   — — — — — —

2. ☐ ☐ ☐ ☐ ☐ ☐
   — — — — — —

3. ☐ ☐ ☐ ☐ ☐
   — — — — —

4. ☐ ☐ ☐
   — — —

Part b

1. _____ 3. _____

2. _____ 4. _____

Part c

☐ ☐ ☐ ☐ ☐ ☐ ☐ ☐ ☐ ☐
— — — — — — — — — —

☐ ☐ ☐ ☐ ☐ .
— — — — —

_____

Part d

Lesson 53

Part a

1. _____   4. _____

2. _____   5. _____

3. _____

Part b

_____

Part c

☐☐ ☐☐ ☐ ☐☐☐☐☐ ☐☐☐ ☐☐☐☐

☐☐ ☐☐ ☐ ☐☐☐.

_____

Part d

Lesson 54

Part a

1. _____ 4. _____

2. _____ 5. _____

3. _____ 6. _____

Part b

1. _____

2. _____

Part c

□□ □ □□ □□ □ □ □ □ □ □

□ □ □ □ □.

_____

Part d

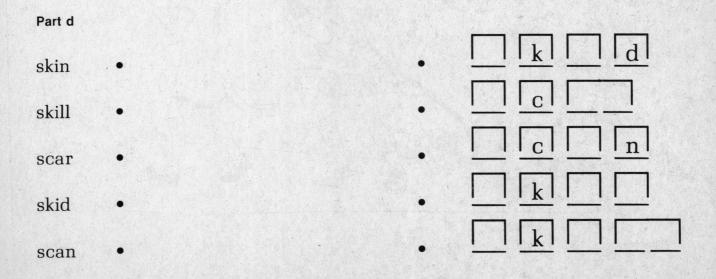

skin •

skill •

scar •

skid •

scan •

Lesson 55

Part a

1. <u>how</u>   2. h<u>owl</u>   3. do<u>wn</u>

Part b

1. _____

2. _____

Part c

how   •   •   [ ] [o] [w] [ ]

leader   •   •   [ ] [ ] [ ] [ ] [ ] [e] [r]

steam   •   •   [ ] [e] [a] [ ] [ ]

scamper   •   •   [ ] [o] [w]

howl   •   •   [ ] [ ] [e] [a] [ ]

Part d

1. _____   8. _____

2. _____   9. _____

3. _____   10. _____

4. _____   11. _____

5. _____   12. _____

6. _____   13. _____

7. _____   14. _____

Lesson 56

Part a

1. h<u>ow</u>   2. h<u>ow</u>l   3. d<u>ow</u>n

Part b

1. _____

2. _____

Part c

We saw these girls beegin.

Part d

1. _____   5. _____

2. _____   6. _____

3. _____   7. _____

4. _____

Part e

Lesson 57

Part a

1. _____

2. _____

Part b

Were the goats eating weads?

Part c

Birds know how to fly south.

_____

Part d

speak   •

trap   •

stem   •

reach   •

true   •

• ☐ e a ☐

• t ☐ ☐

• s ☐ ☐ ☐

• ☐ ☐ a ☐

• s ☐ ☐ ☐

Lesson 58

Part a

1. _____   6. _____

2. _____   7. _____

3. _____   8. _____

4. _____   9. _____

5. _____

Part b

1. _____

2. _____

Part c

◻ i r ◻ ◻ k ◻ ◻ w ◻ ◻

◻ ◻ ◻ ◻ y ◻ o u ◻ .

_____

Part d

Do yue have blue shues ?

Lesson 59

Part a

1. _____
2. _____
3. _____
4. _____
5. _____

6. _____
7. _____
8. _____
9. _____
10. _____

Part b

1. _____
2. _____

Part c

She shud speak up.

Part d

☐ ☐ ☐ ☐ ☐ k ☐ ☐ w ☐ ☐
___ ___ ___ ___ ___ ___ ___ ___ ___ ___ ___

☐ ☐ ☐ ☐ y ☐ o u ☐ .
___ ___ ___ ___ ___ ___ ___ ___ ___

_____

Part e

1. ☐ ☐ i ☐
___ ___ ___ ___

2. ☐ l ☐ ☐
___ ___ ___ ___

3. ☐ ☐ i ☐
___ ___ ___ ___

4. ☐ l ☐ ☐
___ ___ ___ ___

5. ☐ l ☐ ☐
___ ___ ___ ___

Lesson 60

Part a

☐ ☐ ☐ ☐ ☐ k ☐ ☐ w ☐ ☐
☐☐ ☐ ☐ ☐ ☐ o u ☐.

_____

Part b

1. _____   4. _____

2. _____   5. _____

3. _____   6. _____

Part c

1. _____

2. _____

Part d

how   •   •   ☐ o w

prowl   •   •   ☐ r o w l

howl   •   •   h ☐

growl   •   •   ☐ o w l

cow   •   •   p ☐ ☐ ☐

Lesson 61

Part a

1. _____ 5. _____ 9. _____

2. _____ 6. _____ 10. _____

3. _____ 7. _____

4. _____ 8. _____

Part b

1. _____

2. _____

3. _____

Part c

□ □ □ □ □ □ □ □ □ □ □

□ □ □ □ □ □ □ o □ □□ .

_____

Part d

Lesson 62

Part a

1. _____

2. _____

3. _____

4. _____

5. _____

Part b

☐ ☐ ☐ ☐ ☐ ☐ ☐ ☐ ☐ ☐ ☐

☐ ☐ ☐ ☐ ☐ ☐ ☐ ☐ .

_____

Part c

1. _____ 5. _____ 9. _____

2. _____ 6. _____ 10. _____

3. _____ 7. _____ 11. _____

4. _____ 8. _____ 12. _____

Part d

Lesson 63

Part a

1. _____   5. _____

2. _____   6. _____

3. _____   7. _____

4. _____   8. _____

Part b

1. _____

2. _____

3. _____

Part c

Lesson 64

Part a

1. _____

2. _____

Part b

Do you have sum shooz?

Kan he put that uway?

Part c

1. _____   6. _____

2. _____   7. _____

3. _____   8. _____

4. _____   9. _____

5. _____   10. _____

Part d

1.

2.

3.

4.

5.

6.

7.

8.

Lesson 65

Part a

1. _____   6. _____

2. _____   7. _____

3. _____   8. _____

4. _____   9. _____

5. _____   10. _____

Part b

1. _____

2. _____

3. _____

Part c

Lesson 66

Part a

1. _____   5. _____

2. _____   6. _____

3. _____   7. _____

4. _____   8. _____

Part b

1. _____

2. _____

3. _____

Part c

We saw these goats skamper.

Part d

Lesson 67

Part a

1. _____

2. _____

3. _____

Part b

1. _____   6. _____   11. _____

2. _____   7. _____   12. _____

3. _____   8. _____   13. _____

4. _____   9. _____   14. _____

5. _____   10. _____   15. _____

Part c

shout   •　　　　　•　 | s | h | o | u | | |

glad   •　　　　　•　 | g | | | |

ground   •　　　　　•　 | g | | | |

should   •　　　　　•　 | s | h | o | u | |

goats   •　　　　　•　 | g | | | | |

Lesson 68

Part a

1. _____   2. _____   3. _____

Part b

1. _____

2. _____

3. _____

Part c

Lesson 69

Part a

1. _____   2. _____   3. _____

Part b

1. _____

2. _____

3. _____

Part c

1. _____   5. _____

2. _____   6. _____

3. _____   7. _____

4. _____   8. _____

Part d

enough •   • [ ] [o] [u] [g] [h]

repeat •   • [r] [ ] [ ] [ ] [ ]

tough •   • [ ] [ ] [o] [u] [g] [h]

rough •   • [r] [e] [ ] [ ]

real •   • [r] [e] [ ] [ ] [ ]

Lesson 70

Part a

1. _____ 2. _____ 3. _____

Part b

1. _____ 3. _____ 5. _____
2. _____ 4. _____ 6. _____

Part c

1. _____ 2. _____

Part d

_____

Part e

Lesson 71

Part a

1. _____   3. _____   5. _____

2. _____   4. _____   6. _____

Part b

_____

Part c

1. _____   6. _____   11. _____

2. _____   7. _____   12. _____

3. _____   8. _____   13. _____

4. _____   9. _____   14. _____

5. _____   10. _____   15. _____

Part d

Lesson 72

Part a

1. _____
2. _____
3. _____

Part b

Theez cowz are eating weads.

Part c

1. _____   6. _____
2. _____   7. _____
3. _____   8. _____
4. _____   9. _____
5. _____   10. _____

Part d

Lesson 73

Part a

1. _____

2. _____

3. _____

4. _____

Part b

1. _____   5. _____

2. _____   6. _____

3. _____   7. _____

4. _____   8. _____

Part c

sprint •

splash •

scrap •

split •

spring •

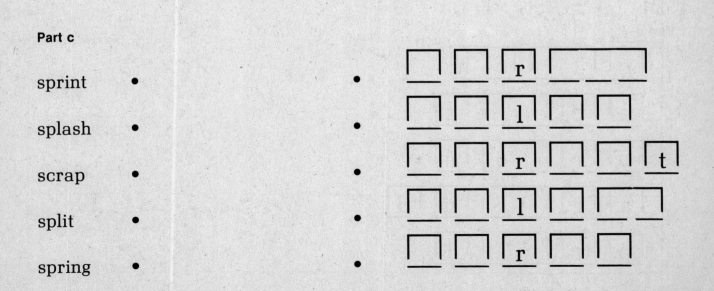

Lesson 74

Part a

1. _____

2. _____

3. _____

Part b

1. Wer the girls going owt **?**

2. Did they eat enuf **?**

Part c

1. _____   6. _____

2. _____   7. _____

3. _____   8. _____

4. _____   9. _____

5. _____   10. _____

Part d

1. c __ __ c h

2. a b __ __ t

3. b r __ __ n

4. a r __ __ n d

5. p r __ __ l

Part a

1. _____   6. _____

2. _____   7. _____

3. _____   8. _____

4. _____   9. _____

5. _____   10. _____

Part b

1. _____

2. _____

Part c

couch •

count •

cloud •

clown •

proud •

• | | | | n | t |

• | c | o | u | | |

• | | | o | u | d |

• | c | l | | | |

• | | | o | w | n |

Lesson 76

Part a

1. _____

2. _____

3. _____

Part b

1. | a | b | ___ | t |

2. | c | ___ | c | h |

3. | c | l | ___ | n |

4. | c | ___ | n | t |

5. | a | r | ___ | n | d |

Part c

Lesson 77

Part a

1. _____

2. _____

3. _____

Part b

I will meet a beetle with green feet.

_____

Part c

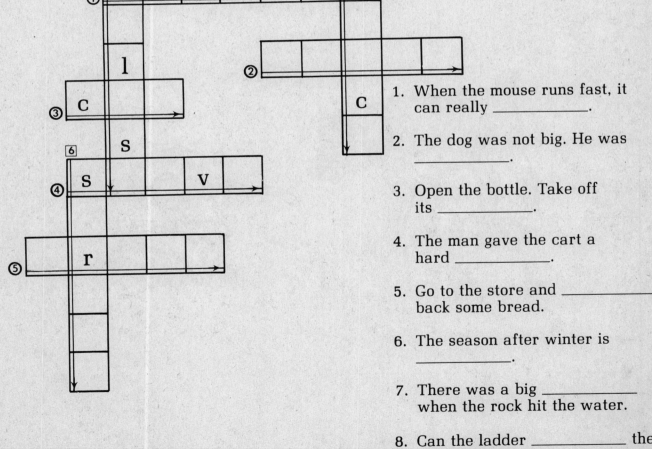

1. When the mouse runs fast, it can really _____.

2. The dog was not big. He was _____.

3. Open the bottle. Take off its _____.

4. The man gave the cart a hard _____.

5. Go to the store and _____ back some bread.

6. The season after winter is _____.

7. There was a big _____ when the rock hit the water.

8. Can the ladder _____ the top of the barn?

Lesson 78

Part a

1. _____   6. _____

2. _____   7. _____

3. _____   8. _____

4. _____   9. _____

5. _____   10. _____

Part b

1. _____

2. _____

Part c

Part d

_____

Part a

1. _____

2. _____

Part b

Did you hear that lowd sownd?

The gurls are reading sum of the book.

Part c

1. _____   4. _____   7. _____

2. _____   5. _____   8. _____

3. _____   6. _____   9. _____

Part d

1. [l] [__] [__]

2. [n] [__] [t]

3. [m] [_ e] [t]

4. [r] [__] [l]

5. [r] [__] [__]

Lesson 80

Part a

1. _____

2. _____

Part b

He said that he wanted to work.

_____

Part c

Part a

1. _____

2. _____

Part b

☐☐ ☐ a i ☐ ☐ ☐ ☐ ☐ ☐ ☐ ☐

w a ☐ ☐ e d ☐ ☐ ☐ o r k .

Part c

Lesson 82

Part a

1. _____

2. _____

3. _____

Part b

Did he have a skar?

Part c

1. bark + _____ = _____   4. splash + _____ = _____

2. fish   + _____ = _____   5. mark + _____ = _____

3. reach + _____ = _____

Part d

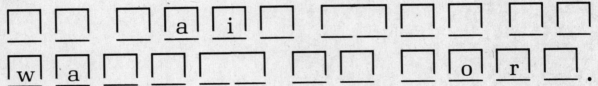

Part e

Lesson 83

Part a

1. _____

2. _____

3. _____

Part b

1. dash   + _____ = _____   4. rush   + _____ = _____

2. reach   + _____ = _____   5. mark   + _____ = _____

3. bark   + _____ = _____

Part c

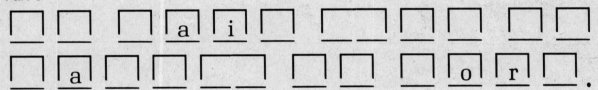

Part d

proud   •

leaf   •

clown   •

prowl   •

cloud   •

•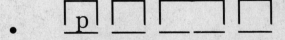

•

•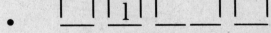

•

•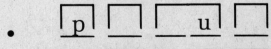

Lesson 84

Part a

1. _____

2. _____

Part b

Will you help me owt **?**

Part c

☐ ☐   ☐ ☐ ☐ ☐   ☐ ☐ ☐ ☐   ☐ ☐

☐ ☐ ☐ ☐ ☐ ☐   ☐ ☐   ☐ ☐o☐ ☐ .

Part d

Lesson 85

Part a

1. _____

2. _____

3. _____

Part b

1. _____   4. _____

2. _____   5. _____

3. _____

Part c

weeds   •

reach   •

read   •

real   •

repeat   •

•   ☐ ☐ d s

•   r e ☐

•   r e ☐ ☐ ☐

•   ☐ ☐ d

•   r e ☐ ☐

Lesson 86

Part a

1. ☐ ☐a☐ ☐s☐ ☐ ☐ ☐

2. ☐ ☐i☐ ☐ ☐ ☐

3. ☐ ☐ ☐a☐ ☐ ☐ ☐ ☐

4. ☐ ☐ ☐ ☐ ☐ ☐ ☐ ☐

5. ☐ ☐a☐ ☐ ☐

Part b

1. _____

2. _____

3. _____

Part c

1. _____   7. _____

2. _____   8. _____

3. _____   9. _____

4. _____   10. _____

5. _____   11. _____

6. _____   12. _____

Lesson 87

Part a

Does that little skunk stink?

_____

Part b

1. my   3. why   5. cry   7. sky   9. dry
2. try   4. by   6. shy   8. ply   10. fly

Part c

He sed that he wanted to call.

Part d

1. _____   5. _____
2. _____   6. _____
3. _____   7. _____
4. _____   8. _____

Part e

_____

Part f

Lesson 88

Part a

1. _____
2. _____
3. _____

4. _____
5. _____

Part b

1. _____
2. _____
3. _____

4. _____
5. _____
6. _____

Part c

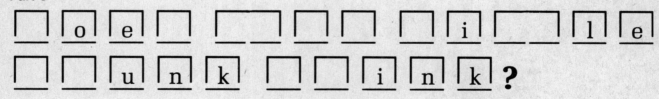

_____

Part d

_____

Lesson 89

Part a

1. _____
2. _____
3. _____
4. _____

5. _____
6. _____
7. _____
8. _____

9. _____
10. _____
11. _____

Part b

| □ | o | e | □ | □ | □ | □ | □ | i | □ | □ | l | e |

| □ | □ | □ | □ | □ | □ | □ |
|s|k| | | |s|t| | | | **?**

_____

Part c

1. _____
2. _____

Part d

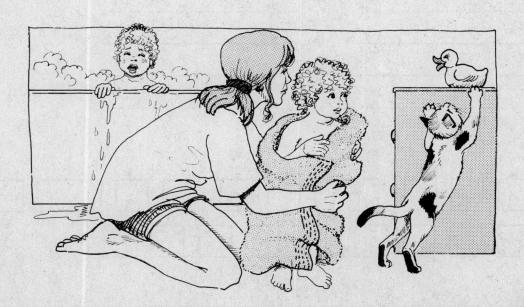

Lesson 90

Part a

1. _____ + _____ = _____

2. _____ + _____ = _____

3. _____ + _____ = _____

4. _____ + _____ = _____

5. _____ + _____ = _____

Part b

1. _____

2. _____

3. _____

Part c

1. high   2. sigh

Part d

1. _____   6. _____

2. _____   7. _____

3. _____   8. _____

4. _____   9. _____

5. _____   10. _____

Part e

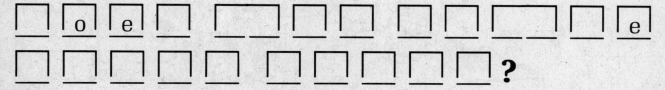

Lesson 91

Part a

1. high   2. sigh

Part b

□ □ □ □ □ □ □ □ □ □ □ □ □

□ □ □ □ □ □ □ □ □ □ **?**

_____

Part c

_____

Part d

Lesson 92

Part a

1. _____   5. _____

2. _____   6. _____

3. _____   7. _____

4. _____   8. _____

Part b

1. _____

2. _____

Part c

Birds know how to fly hy.

Part d

□ □ □ □ □ □ □ □ □ □ □ □ □ □

□ □ □ □ □ □ □ □ □ □ **?**

_____

Part e

why •   • [□ h □]

high •   • [s □ □]

sky •   • [w □ □]

sigh •   • [□ i g h]

sh, •   • [s □ □]

Lesson 93

Part a

1. where   2. there   3. here

Part b

1. _____

2. _____

Part c

1. _____   5. _____

2. _____   6. _____

3. _____   7. _____

4. _____   8. _____

Part d

Lesson 94

Part a

1. _____   6. _____

2. _____   7. _____

3. _____   8. _____

4. _____   9. _____

5. _____   10. _____

Part b

1. _____

2. _____

3. _____

Part c

1. _____   2. _____   3. _____

Part d

there •

where •

were •

here •

thank •

• | t | | | |

• | | | e | r | e |

• | w | | | |

• | | | | |

• | w | | | |

Lesson 95

Part a

1. _____
2. _____
3. _____

4. _____
5. _____

Part b

1. _____
2. _____

Part c

Part a

That little boy duz try.

Part b

1. sink   4. drink

2. sank   5. drank

3. sunk   6. drunk

Part c

Lesson 97

Part a

1. _____

2. _____

Part b

Can I have sum of thoze?

Part c

1. _____   4. _____

2. _____   5. _____

3. _____   6. _____

Part d

Lesson 98

Part a

1. _____   4. _____

2. _____   5. _____

3. _____

Part b

1. _____   4. _____

2. _____   5. _____

3. _____   6. _____

Part c

1. _____

2. _____

Part d

Lesson 99

Part a

Which is your home?

_____

Part b

1. _____

2. _____

3. _____

4. _____

Part c

Do ouls know how to fligh?

Part d

there   •

these   •

those   •

here   •

where   •

•

•

•

•

•

		e	r	e
t	h			
			s	e
		o		

Lesson 100

Part a

W h ☐ ☐ ☐ ☐☐ ☐☐☐ r
☐ ☐ ☐ e ?

_____

Part b

1. _____

2. _____

Part c

1. should   2. could   3. would

Part d

1. _____   6. _____

2. _____   7. _____

3. _____   8. _____

4. _____   9. _____

5. _____   10. _____

Part e

Lesson 101

Part a

1. _____

2. _____

3. _____

Part b

1. _____

2. _____

3. _____

Part c

He sed that he will trigh.

Part d

☐☐☐☐ ☐☐ ☐☐☐☐
☐☐☐☐ **?**

_____

Part e

1. _____

2. _____

3. _____

4. _____

5. _____

6. _____

7. _____

8. _____

9. _____

10. _____

11. _____

12. _____

Lesson 102

Part a

☐ ☐ ☐ ☐ ☐ ☐ ☐ ☐ ☐
☐ ☐ ☐ ☐ **?**

_____

Part b

1. _____

2. _____

Part c

Did you get that job dun **?**

Part d

Lesson 103

Part a

1. _____

2. _____

Part b

1. _____   5. _____   9. _____

2. _____   6. _____   10. _____

3. _____   7. _____

4. _____   8. _____

Part c

1. _____   2. _____   3. _____

Part d

May I have some gloo?

Part e

□□ □ □   □ □   □ □ □ □

□ □ □ □ **?**

Part f

Lesson 104

Part a

1. _____

2. _____

3. _____

Part b

1. _____   6. _____

2. _____   7. _____

3. _____   8. _____

4. _____   9. _____

5. _____

Part c

Lesson 105

Part a

1. _____

2. _____

Part b

1. _____   6. _____

2. _____   7. _____

3. _____   8. _____

4. _____   9. _____

5. _____   10. _____

Part c

Lesson 106

Part a

1. _____

2. _____

Part b

I thought he was through.

_____

Part c

1. _____   4. _____

2. _____   5. _____

3. _____   6. _____

Part d

Lesson 107

Part a

[ ] [ ] o u g h [ ] [ ] [ ] [ ] a s
t h [ ] o u g h .

_____

Part b

1. _____

2. _____

Part c

1. _____   6. _____

2. _____   7. _____

3. _____   8. _____

4. _____   9. _____

5. _____   10. _____

Part d

then   •   •   [ ] [ ] e [ ]

them   •   •   t h [ ] [ ] [ ]

than   •   •   [ ] [ ] n

there   •   •   [ ] [ ] e r e

where   •   •   [ ] [ ] a [ ]

Part a

Part b

Wud you like a drink **?**

Part c

☐ t h ☐ ☐ ☐ ☐ ☐   ☐ ☐   ☐ ☐ ☐

☐ ☐ ☐ o u g h .

Part d

1. _____   6. _____

2. _____   7. _____

3. _____   8. _____

4. _____   9. _____

5. _____   10. _____

Lesson 109

Part a

1. _____

2. _____

3. _____

4. _____

Part b

☐ ☐☐☐☐☐☐ ☐☐ ☐ ☐☐ ☐
☐☐☐☐☐☐ .

_____

Part c

1. Her room looked very
   _____ and clean.

2. His voice was so hoarse
   he could not _____.

3. The boy always got what
   he _____.

4. Can you tell me
   _____ it is ?

5. We don't want two. We
   only want _____.

6. Wash the dishes in the
   kitchen _____.

7. Don't take those books.
   Take _____ books.

8. Whatever goes up must
   come _____.

9. The pen was filled with
   _____.

10. Come over _____
    right away.

Lesson 110

Part a

1. _____

2. _____

3. _____

Part b

1. _____   4. _____

2. _____   5. _____

3. _____   6. _____

Part c

□ □ □ □ □ □ □ □ □ □ □ □

□ □ □ □ □ □ .

_____

Part d

Lesson 111

Part a

1. _____   5. _____

2. _____   6. _____

3. _____   7. _____

4. _____

Part b

1. _____

2. _____

Part c

□ □□□□□□ □□ □□□
□□□□□□.

_____

Part d

1. w □ □ □ □

2. w □ □ l

3. n □ □

4. t h □ □ □

5. □ a r k □ □

Lesson 112

He writes better than he talks.

_____

Part b

1. _____   5. _____

2. _____   6. _____

3. _____   7. _____

4. _____   8. _____

Part c

1. _____

2. _____

3. _____

Part d

1. | s | | | |

2. | | | |

3. | n | | | |

4. | s | | | | | |

5. | | | |

Part a

☐ ☐ ☐ r i ☐ e s ☐ ☐ t e r

☐ ☐ ☐ ☐ ☐ ☐ a l k ☐ .

Part b

1. _____

2. _____

Part c

Even he cood do that.

Part d

1. _____   6. _____

2. _____   7. _____

3. _____   8. _____

4. _____   9. _____

5. _____   10. _____

Part a

□ □ □ r i □ e □ □ □ □ er
□ □ □ □ □ □ □ a l □ □ .

_____

Part b

1. _____
2. _____
3. _____

Part c

He should not have wun of thoze.

Part d

Lesson 115

Part a

1. _____
2. _____
3. _____

Part b

1. _____ 4. _____

2. _____ 5. _____

3. _____

Part c

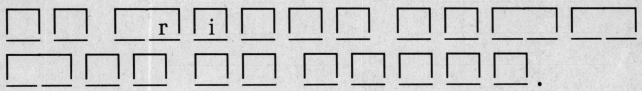

_____

Part d

1.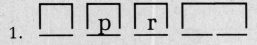

2.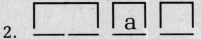

3.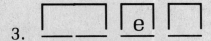

4.

5.

Lesson 116

Part a

□□ □□□□□ □□□□□
□□□ □□ □□□□□.

_____

Part b

1. _____   14. _____
2. _____   15. _____
3. _____   15. _____
4. _____   17. _____
5. _____   18. _____
6. _____   19. _____
7. _____   20. _____
8. _____   21. _____
9. _____   22. _____
10. _____   23. _____
11. _____   24. _____
12. _____   25. _____
13. _____

Lesson 117

Part a

I wonder why the city is quiet.

_____

Part b

1. _____   4. _____

2. _____   5. _____

3. _____

Part c

1. _____

2. _____

Part d

Lesson 118

Part a

1. might   3. right   5. light
2. flight   4. tight   6. bright

Part b

1. _____

2. _____

Part c

☐ ☐ o ☐ ☐ ☐ ☐ ☐ ☐ ☐ ☐ ☐ ☐ ☐

c ☐ ☐ y ☐ ☐ q u ☐ e t .

Part d

Lesson 119

Part a

☐ ☐ o ☐ ☐ ☐ ☐ ☐ ☐ ☐ ☐ ☐
☐ c ☐ ☐ y ☐ ☐ ☐ ☐ e t .

_____

Part b

1. fight   2. light   3. night

Part c

1. _____

2. _____

3. _____

Part d

1. Things aren't getting worse. They're getting _____.

2. He said "No," and _____ his head.

3. The board is not smooth. It is _____.

4. The dog started to bark and _____.

5. She lives very far _____.

6. Who is mayor of that _____?

7. Tiny drops of water are called a _____.

8. The thread went _____ the hole of the needle.

9. After the meeting, they all went _____.

10. There are 365 days in a _____.

Lesson 120

Part a

□ □ □□□□ □□ □□ □□ □

□ □□ y □□ □ □□□□.

_____

Part b

1. _____

2. _____

Part c

1. _____   4. _____

2. _____   5. _____

3. _____

Part d

Lesson 121

Part a

1. _____
2. _____
3. _____

4. _____
5. _____
6. _____

Part b

_____

Part c

1. _____
2. _____

Part d

1. [s] [ ] [ ]
2. [t] [ ] [ ]
3. [b] [l] [ ] [ ]
4. [d] [r] [ ] [ ]
5. [s] [k] [ ] [ ]

Lesson 122

Part a

1. _____
2. _____
3. _____
4. _____
5. _____
6. _____
7. _____
8. _____
9. _____
10. _____

Part b

1. _____
2. _____
3. _____
4. _____
5. _____

Part c

sigh   •

fly   •

sight   •

fight   •

flight   •

• [ ] [i] [g] [h] [ ]

• [f] [ ] [ ] [ ]

• [s] [ ] [ ]

• [ ] [ ] [i] [g] [h] [ ]

• [f] [ ] [ ]

Lesson 123

Part a

1. _____   4. _____

2. _____   5. _____

3. _____   6. _____

Part b

1. _____

2. _____

Part c

She didn't listen to anybody.

_____

Part d

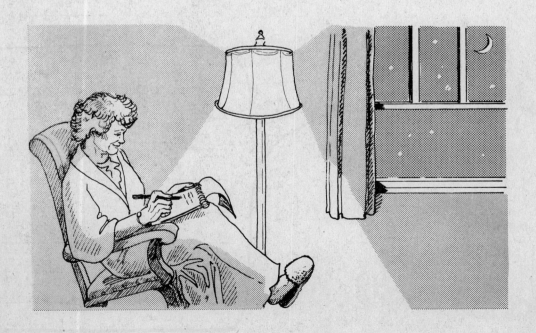

Lesson 124

Part a

1. _____   5. _____

2. _____   6. _____

3. _____   7. _____

4. _____

Part b

1. _____

2. _____

Part c

⬚ ⬚ ⬚ ⬚ ⬚ ⬚ n't ⬚ ⬚ ⬚ t e ⬚

⬚ ⬚ a ⬚ y b o ⬚ y .

_____

Part d

Part a

☐☐ ☐ ☐☐☐ n't ☐ i s ☐☐ ☐

☐☐ ☐☐☐ b o ☐☐ .

_____

Part b

1. _____ 4. _____

2. _____ 5. _____

3. _____ 6. _____

Part c

1. _____

2. _____

3. _____

4. _____

Part d

fly   •   • ☐ f ☐ l ☐☐☐ ☐

sigh   •   • s ☐ ☐

sight   •   • ☐ ☐ y

flight   •   • s i g h ☐

sly   •   • s ☐

Lesson 126

Part a

1. _____   3. _____

2. _____   4. _____

Part b

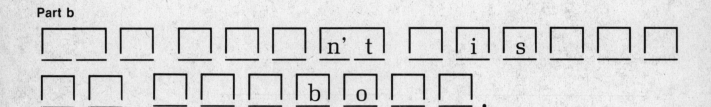

_____

Part c

1. _____

2. _____

Part d

fly   •   • [___] [y]

light   •   • [f] [_] [___] [_]

flight   •   • [f] [___] [_]

why   •   • [_] [i] [g] [h] [_]

fight   •   • [f] [_] [_]

Lesson 127

Part a

1. _____

2. _____

Part b

1. _____   5. _____

2. _____   6. _____

3. _____   7. _____

4. _____

Part c

⬜⬜ ⬜ ⬜ ⬜ ⬜ ⬜ ⬜ ⬜ ⬜ ⬜ ⬜ ⬜ ⬜
⬜⬜ ⬜ ⬜⬜ ⬜ ⬜ ⬜ ⬜ ⬜ ⬜ ⬜.

_____

Part d

Lesson 128

Part a

1. _____   5. _____

2. _____   6. _____

3. _____   7. _____

4. _____

Part b

1. _____

2. _____

Part c

Lesson 129

Part a

1. _____ 6. _____
2. _____ 7. _____
3. _____ 8. _____
4. _____ 9. _____
5. _____ 10. _____

Part b

1. _____
2. _____
3. _____
4. _____
5. _____

Part c

Lesson 130

Part a

1. _____

2. _____

Part b

1. _____   4. _____

2. _____   5. _____

3. _____

Part c

I believe he lost every race.

_____

Part d

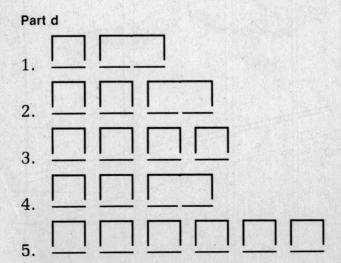

Part a

☐ ☐☐ ☐i ☐e ☐e☐ ☐☐
☐ ☐o☐ ☐ ☐☐ ☐er y ☐☐ ☐ce .

_____

Part b

1. _____   4. _____

2. _____   5. _____

3. _____

Part c

grape •   • ☐s ☐ ☐

cape •   • ☐c ☐ ☐

stay •   • ☐ ☐ a☐ p☐ e☐

play •   • ☐ a☐ p☐ e☐

clay •   • ☐ ☐ a☐ y

Part d

1. _____   6. _____   11. _____

2. _____   7. _____   12. _____

3. _____   8. _____   13. _____

4. _____   9. _____   14. _____

5. _____   10. _____   15. _____

Lesson 132

Part a

1. _____

2. _____

3. _____

Part b

☐ ☐ ☐ ☐ i ☐ ☐ e ☐ ☐

☐ o ☐ ☐ ☐ ☐ e r ☐ ☐ ☐ c ☐ .

_____

Part c

Lesson 133

Part a

1. _____

2. _____

Part b

1. _____   4. _____

2. _____   5. _____

3. _____   6. _____

Part c

☐ ☐ ☐ ☐ i ☐ e ☐ ☐

☐ o ☐ ☐ ☐ ☐ e r ☐ ☐ ☐ c ☐ .

Part d

Lesson 134

Part a

1. _____   4. _____

2. _____   5. _____

3. _____

Part b

1. _____

2. _____

Part c

☐ ☐ ☐ ☐ ☐ ☐ ☐☐ ☐☐

☐ ☐ ☐ ☐ ☐ ☐ ☐☐ ☐ ☐ ☐ ☐ .

_____

Part d

torch •

pork •

fork •

porch •

port •

Lesson 135

Part a

People watched from the other building.

_____

Part b

1. _____
2. _____
3. _____
4. _____

Part c

1. _____   9. _____
2. _____   10. _____
3. _____   11. _____
4. _____   12. _____
5. _____   13. _____
6. _____   14. _____
7. _____   15. _____
8. _____

Part a

1. _____

2. _____

3. _____

Part b

□ e o □ □ e   □ a t _ _ □   □ □ o □   □ □

o □ □ □   □ u □ □ □ □ _ .

_____

Part c

sport •   • □ □ □ n

coin •   • □ p o r □

born •   • □ o r □

spoil •   • □ o i n

porch •   • s p □ □ □

Lesson 137

Part a

1. _____

2. _____

3. _____

Part b

1. _____   3. _____

2. _____   4. _____

Part c

☐ e o ☐ ☐ e ☐ a t ☐ ☐ ☐ ☐ o ☐ ☐ ☐
o ☐ ☐ ☐ ☐ u ☐ ☐ ☐ ☐ .

_____

Part d

Lesson 138

Part a

1. _____
2. _____
3. _____
4. _____

Part b

1. _____   4. _____

2. _____   5. _____

3. _____

Part c

☐ ☐ o ☐ ☐ e ☐ a t ☐ ☐ ☐ ☐ o ☐ ☐ ☐
o ☐ ☐ ☐ ☐ u ☐ ☐ ☐ ☐ ☐ .

Part d

Lesson 139

Part a

1. _____

2. _____

3. _____

4. _____

Part b

☐ ☐ o ☐ ☐ ☐   ☐ a ☐ ☐ ☐ ☐   ☐ ☐ ☐ ☐   ☐ ☐ ☐
☐ ☐ ☐ ☐   ☐ u ☐ ☐ ☐ ☐ ☐ .

_____

Part c

Lesson 140

Part a

1. _____
2. _____
3. _____
4. _____
5. _____
6. _____

Part b

1. _____
2. _____
3. _____
4. _____
5. _____

6. _____
7. _____
8. _____
9. _____
10. _____

11. _____
12. _____
13. _____
14. _____
15. _____

Part c

□ □ □ □ □ □ □ □_□ □ □ □ □ □ □ □
□ □ □ □ □ □ □ □ □_□ .

Part d